Introductory

CELLIS A WHEELS™

Chinese Characters Visual Organiser

W. Q. BLOSH

Introductory Cellis Wheels
Chinese Characters Visual Organiser
W.Q. BLOSH

FIRST EDITION

Written and designed by W.Q. BLOSH

Email: celliswheel@gmail.com
Website: http://celliswheel.com/

ISBN: 978-981-11-6546-7

Printed by IngramSparks

PDF eBOOK available at https://gum.co/ymnMl

CONTENT

How Cellis Wheels™ Work?

Cellis Wheel™

A **Ferris Wheel** is an upright wheel with cabins attached to the rim and connected to the hub (centre) by spokes. It rotates clockwise or anti-clockwise vertically. At first glance, a **Cellis Wheel™** (CW) resembles the Ferris Wheel in many ways—an upright wheel with coloured balls attached to the rim and connected to the centre by spokes.

A CW is much more meaningful, it adapts to the Cell Family that resides within it. The number of cabins depends on the number of members in this family. In addition, all CWs share these common features:

Hub: CELL

The hub contains the CELL, which is a character (or parts of character) that multiplies itself by combining with other parts to form MULTIPLES. The cell is usually enclosed in a **blue ball**.

If it is enclosed in a **black ball**, this means that the cell is <u>not</u> a character. Instead, the cell is made of the common parts that all the other multiples in this CW have. As such, this cell does <u>not</u> have a sound.

Balls: MULTIPLES

The MULTIPLES are enclosed in coloured balls at the rim of the wheel. The colour of the balls indicate the sound of the multiples in relation to the sound of the CELL.

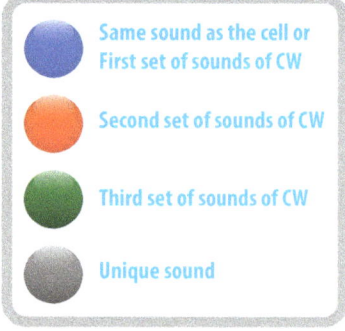

- Same sound as the cell or First set of sounds of CW
- Second set of sounds of CW
- Third set of sounds of CW
- Unique sound

Multiple = CELL + Parts

Each MULTIPLE is made up of the CELL (shown in white font) and other parts (shown in yellow font).

CELL   MULTIPLE

Orientation: Clockwise ONLY

Navigating around the wheel is easy as it only rotates clockwise, and starts at the 12 o'clock position or the 9 o'clock position for CW with only 3 multiples.

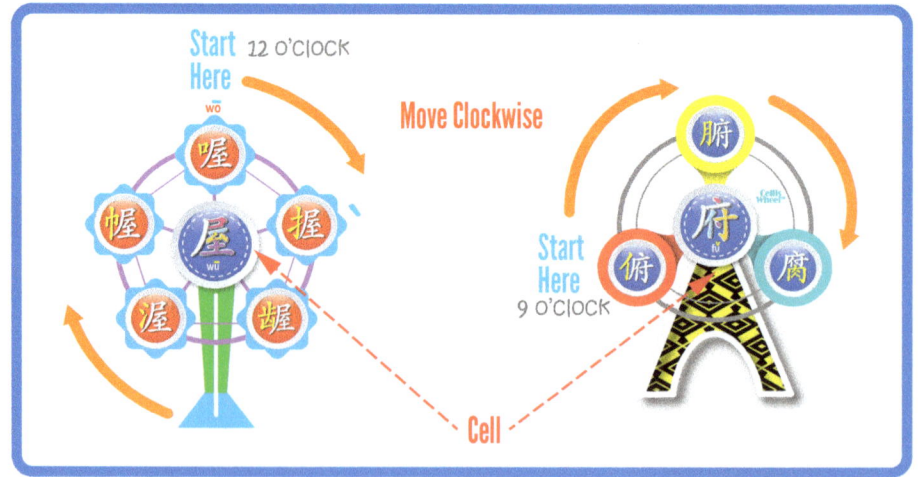

Types of Cellis Wheels™

Unique Wheels

Cellis Wheels™ (CWs) are interesting as each one is unique with their own unique idiosyncrasies. They represent different Cell Families. The size of the wheel varies depending on the number of multiples (minimum of 3 to more than 20). Some CWs are monotonous with only blue balls while others are colourful, carrying multi-coloured balls.

Sound Complexity

The diagram below shows a way to introduce the types of CWs, based on the sound complexities of the characters. A homogeneous Cell Family has characters that share the same sound and tone, hence the CW it creates is a '100% OSOT' (One Sound One Tone).

The sound profile of the Cell Families gets more complex when they form CWs that are OSDT (One Sound Different Tone), RS (Rhyming Sounds), ... (see description below).

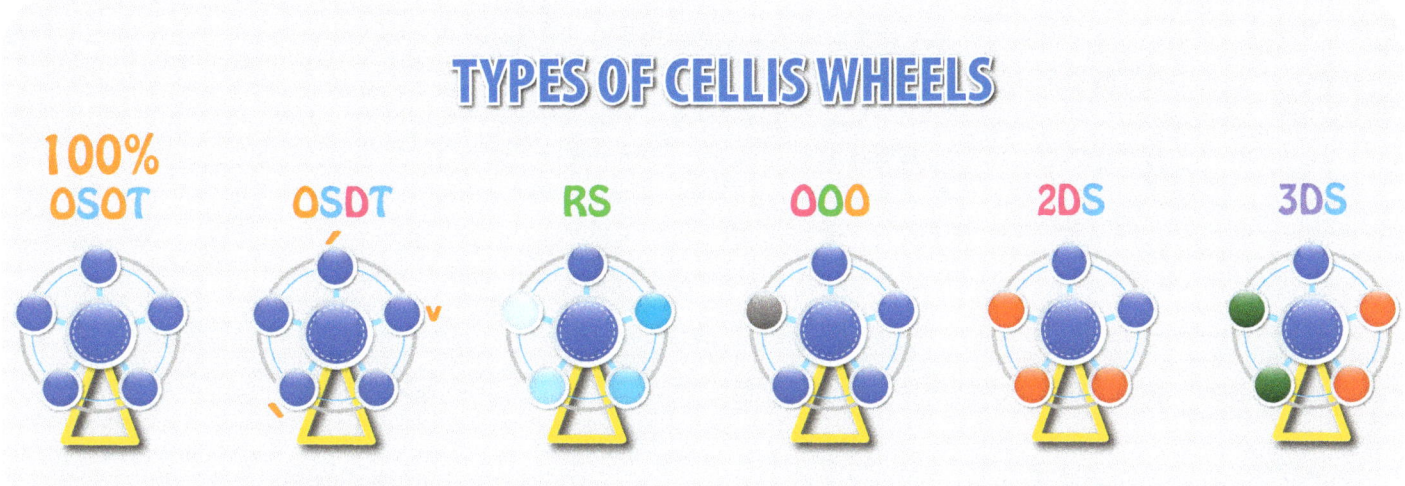

TYPES OF CELLIS WHEELS

100%
OSOT
All characters have the same sound and tone.
Blue balls only, no tone marks

One Sound Different Tone
All characters share the same sound but pronounced in different tones. Take note of **tone marks** besides the blue balls

Rhyming Sounds
Similar-sounding characters that rhyme are enclosed in balls with different shades of **blue**

Odd One Out
Character(s) with unique sound(s) are enclosed in **grey** ball(s)

2 Different Sounds
Characters with a second set of sound are enclosed in **orange** balls

3 Different Sounds
Characters with a third set of sound are enclosed in **green** balls.

Complex CWs can have a combination of these features. For example, OSDT + RS + OOO.

NOTE: CWs with more than 3 different sounds (3DS) are not shown in this book.

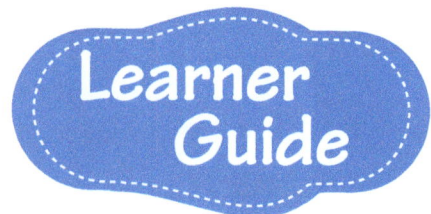

Trick 1 — Guess the Meaning of Characters

Learn how you can guess the meaning of characters by observing the components of the characters

Trick 2 — Learn the Sound of Characters in each CW

Learn the pronunciation of characters more effectively from a CW when you are able to to observe the relationships between the characters

1. Learn the **sound of CELL**

2. Take note of the **type of CW** (see previous page). If the CW is a/an

A) 100% OSOT:
Apply the **sound of CELL** to **ALL** the multiples

B) OSDT:
Vary the tone of the sound when you come across a **different tone mark** as you move clockwise round the wheel

C) RS:
Vary the sound of a multiple when you come across a ball in a **lighter shade of blue.**
Note the similarities and differences in the Hanyin pinyin (*e.g. zhong, chong, cong*)

D) OOO:
Take note of the **unique sound(s)** of multiples in **grey ball(s)** and compare with the sound of the cell

E) 2DS:
Take note of the **second set of sounds (orange balls)** and compare with the sounds of the blue family

F) 3DS:
Take note of the **second and third set of sounds (green balls)** and compare these 3 sets of sounds

Trick 3 — Learn and revise Vocabulary

Apply the characters you have learnt to build new vocabulary. Revise the vocabularies online section by section.

LEARN
1. **Listen** to the Chinese pronunciation
2. **Repeat** what you hear
3. **Understand and remember** the meaning of vocabularies through the English translation and picture (if applicable)

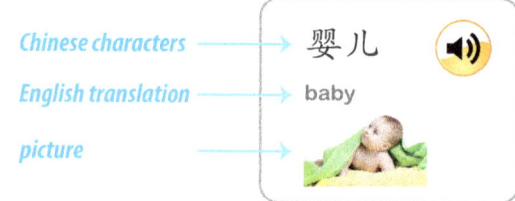

Chinese characters → 婴儿

English translation → baby

picture

FLASHCARDS

1. **Listen** to English translation and **look at** the picture
2. **Recall** the Chinese pronunciation

3. Tap to flip the Flashcard
4. **Listen** to Chinese pronunciation and correct your own pronunciation

MATCH

1. **Revise** all the vocabularies by playing the **Matching Game** in the shortest possible time

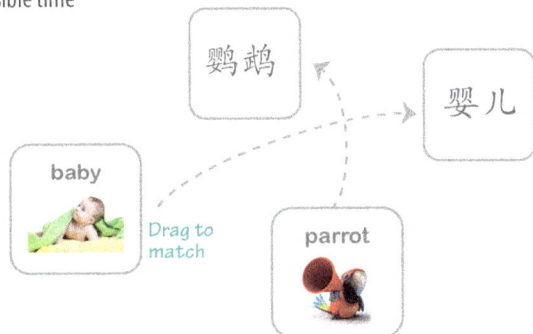

 **Trick 4**

Consolidate
Recall the sounds of each Cellis Wheel

Consolidate what you have learnt after you have completed activities in the book and online. Group characters sharing the same sound within each CW.

 **Trick 5**

'Write' the Characters
Learn to write the characters in your mind.

CELL

Observe the colours of the PARTS in the cell. The character is 'written' in the sequence as shown by the **Part Order Colour Code** - pink, white, blue, yellow, purple, green.

MULTIPLES

'Write' multiples according to the Part Order Structure shown—Left first, followed by right.

Learn more about Part Order and structures of characters in the books ***'Learn Chinese Without Writing 2 and 3'.***

Mix-&-Match
Activity

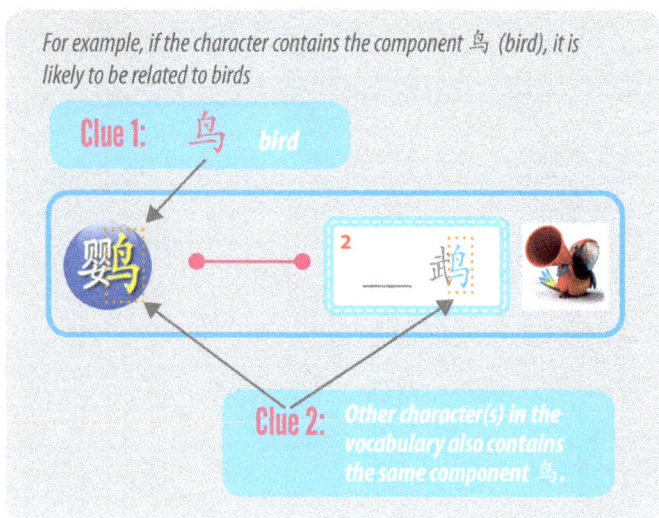

Trick 1

For example, if the character contains the component 鸟 (bird), it is likely to be related to birds

Clue 1: 鹦 — bird

2 ___ 鹉

Clue 2: Other character(s) in the vocabulary also contains the same component 鸟.

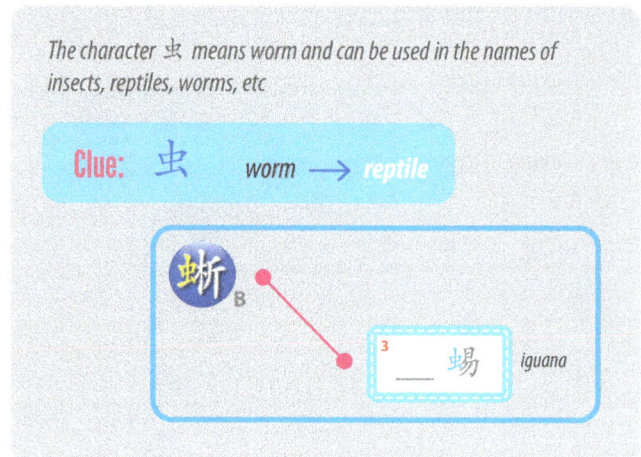

Guess the Meaning of Characters
Guess the meaning of characters by observing the components of the characters

The character 虫 means worm and can be used in the names of insects, reptiles, worms, etc

Clue: 虫 — worm → reptile

3 ___ 蜴 — iguana

蜥 B

Mix-and-Match

缨 A

鹦 B

樱 C

罂 D

1 ___ 桃

2 ___ 鹉

3 ___ 子 — tassel

4 ___ 粟花 — poppy

Mix-and-Match

淅 A

蜥 B

晰 C

晰 D

1 清 ___ — clear, vivid, distinct

2 白 ___ — fair (complexion)

3 ___ 蜴 — iguana

4 ___ — whistling (of wind, rain and snow)

Clues

白 white | 木 wood → plant | 纟 silk → cloth-made stuff

鸟 bird | 氵 water | 虫 worm → reptile | 日 sun → bright → clear

---

2   **ACTIVITY**

Mix-and-Match

 腐 A

 俯 B

 腑 C

1 ___ 冲   *to make a nosedive*

2 脏 ___   *internal organs*

3 豆 ___   *beancurd; tofu*

Mix-and-Match

 拷 A

铐 B

烤 C

1 ___ 炉   *oven*

2 ___ 打   *flog; beat; torture*

3 手 ___   *handcuffs*

Mix-and-Match

 栏 A

 拦 B

 烂 C

1 阻 ___   *to obstruct*

2 ___ 杆   *fence; railing*

3 腐 ___   *to rot; rotten*

Mix-and-Match

 唥 A

 廊 B

 螂 C

 榔 D

1 当 ___   *clang (metallic sound)*

2 走 ___   *corridor*

3 槟 ___   *betel nut*

4 蟑 ___   *cockroach*

Clues

钅	gold → *metal stuff*	木	wood → *wooden stuff*	肉	meat → *food*
广	house on cliff → *place*	木	wood → *plant*	月	flesh → *body part* → *internal organ*
虫	worm → *insect*	虫	worm → *insect*	扌	hand → *action*
口	mouth → *sound*	口	mouth → *sound*	火	fire → *to burn* → *to rot*

Mix-and-Match

A C

踩 A
彩 B
眯 C
菜 D

1  ___踏 — *to trample*
2  蔬___ — *vegetables*
3  ___色笔 — *colour pen*
4 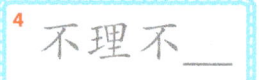 不理不___ — *to ignore*

Mix-and-Match

咦 A
胰 B
痍 C
姨 D

1  阿___ — *auntie*
2  ___ — *huh (express amazement, surprise)*
3  ___脏 — *pancreas*
4  满目疮___ — *scene of devastation*

Mix-and-Match

啰 A
箩 B
萝 C
锣 D
逻 E

1  ___辑 — *logic*
2  ___筐 — *large woven basket*
3  铜___ — *gong*
4  ___嗦 — *long-winded*
4  ___卜 — *carrot*

Mix-and-Match

黛 A
贷 B
袋 C

1  ___子 — *bag; sack*
2  ___款 — *to take a loan; to lend someone money*
3  ___ — *black pigment used to colour eyebrows [ancient]*

Clues

疒 *sickness*
女 *female*
黑 *black*

钅 *gold* → *metal stuff*
𧾷 *foot* → *action (feet)*
目 *eye* → *to see, look*
口 *mouth* → *sound*

贝 *shell* → *money*
纟 *silk* → *cloth-made stuff*
⺮ *bamboo* → *bamboo-made stuff*

艹 *grass* → *plant* → *vegetables*
月 *flesh* → *body part* → *internal organ*
衣 *clothes* → *cloth* → *cloth-made stuff*

4   **ACTIVITY**

OSOT
One Sound One Tone

All the characters in the Cellis Wheel are pronounced in only one way—same sound and same tone.
They are encased in blue balls.

 **Trick 2**
1. Learn the **sound of CELL**
2. Apply the **sound of CELL** to **ALL** the multiples

yīng

1
婴儿
yīng ér
baby

2
樱桃
yīng táo
cherries

樱

5
缨子
yīng zi
tassel

缨

婴
yīng

Cellis Wheel™

鹦鹉

3
鹦鹉
yīng wǔ
parrot

4
罂粟花
yīng sù huā
poppy

罂

1

夷为平地
yí wéi píng dì
raze to the ground

yí

5

满目疮痍
mǎn mù chuāng yí
scene of devastation

2

阿姨
ā yí
auntie

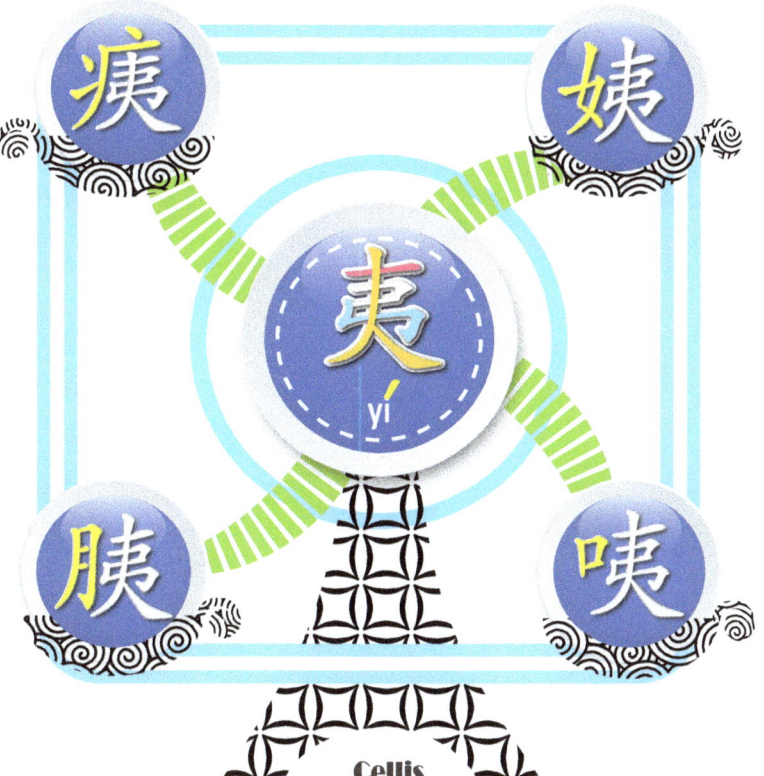

3

咦
yí
huh
(express amazement, surprise)

4

胰脏
yí zàng
pancreas

xī

1
分析
fēn xī
analyse

2
白皙
bái xī
fair (complexion)

3
蜥蜴
xī yì
iguana

5
清晰
qīng xī
clear, vivid, distinct

4
淅淅
xī xī
whistling (of wind, rain and snow)

晰 皙 淅 蜥

析
xī

Cellis Wheel™

dài

1

代替
dài tì
replace;
substitute

2

袋子
dài zi
bag; sack

Cellis
Wheel™

3

贷款
dài kuǎn
to take a loan;
to lend someone
money

4

黛
dài
black pigment used
to colour eyebrows
[ancient];
(used in names)

1

政府
zhèng fǔ
government

2

俯冲
fǔ chōng
*to make a
nosedive*

3

脏腑
zàng fǔ
internal organs

4

豆腐
dòu fu
beancurd; tofu

Cellis
Wheel™

OSDT
One Sound Different Tones

These Cellis Wheels test your musical talents to vary the tone of the
same sound in 4 different ways, indicated by these tone marks:

1st tone: 3rd tone:

2nd tone:    4th tone:

Move clockwise round the wheel and take note of
the change in tone when a new tone mark appears.

1. Learn the **sound of CELL**
2. **Vary the tone** of the sound when you come
across a **different tone mark** as you move
clockwise around the wheel

1

兰花
lán huā
orchid

2

阻拦
zǔ lán
to obstruct

3

栏杆
lán gān
fence; railing

4

腐烂
fǔ làn
to rot; rotten

栏

拦

兰
lán

烂

Cellis
Wheel™

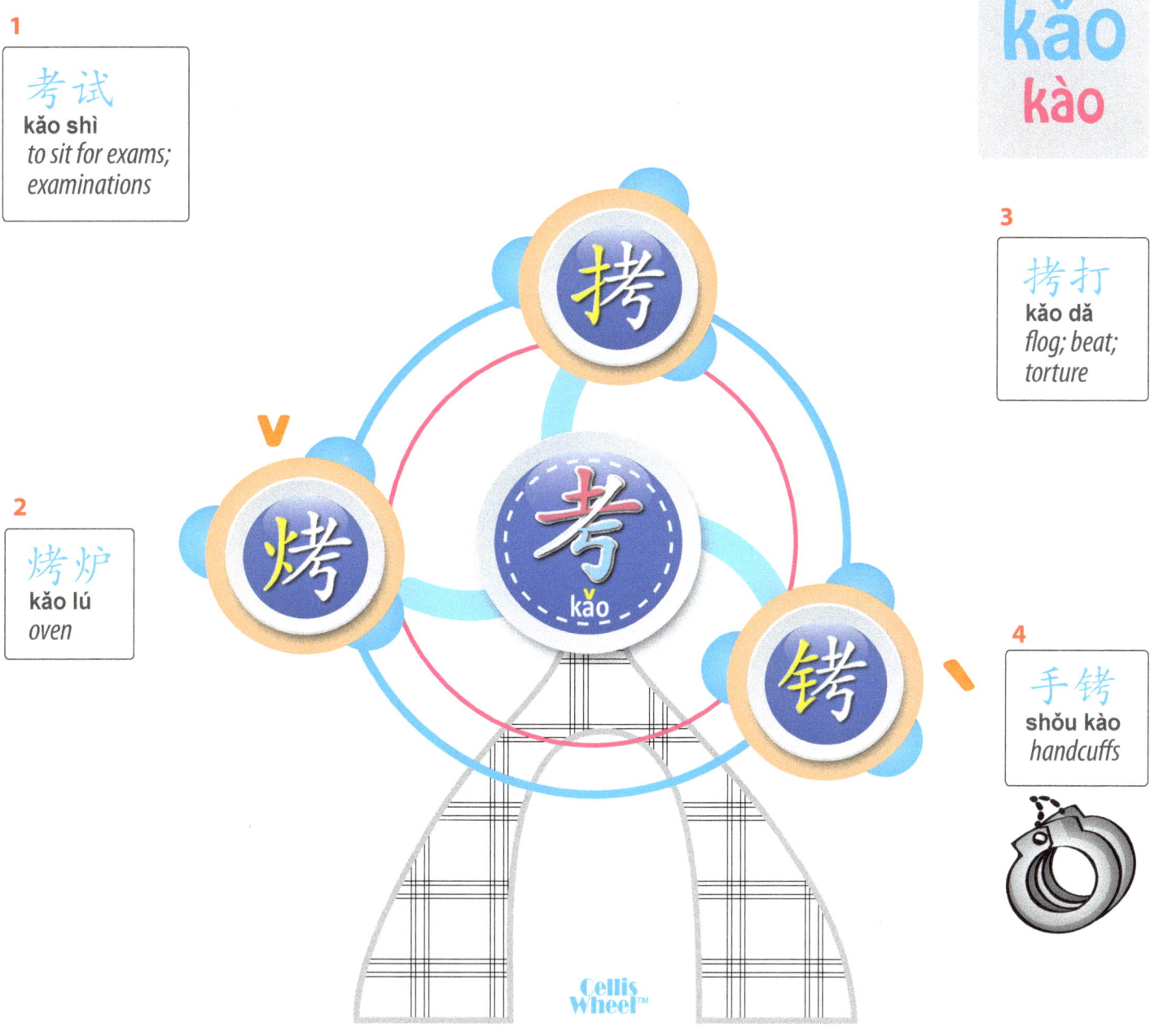

kǎo
kào

1
考试
kǎo shì
to sit for exams; examinations

2
烤炉
kǎo lú
oven

3
拷打
kǎo dǎ
flog; beat; torture

4
手铐
shǒu kào
handcuffs

拷

烤

考
kǎo

铐

Cellis Wheel™

láng
lāng

1
新郎
xīn láng
bridegroom

2
当啷
dāng lāng
clang (metallic sound)

3
走廊
zǒu láng
corridor

4
蟑螂
zhāng láng
cockroach

5
槟榔
bīng lang
betel nut

郎
láng

榔　嘟
螂　廊

Cellis Wheel™

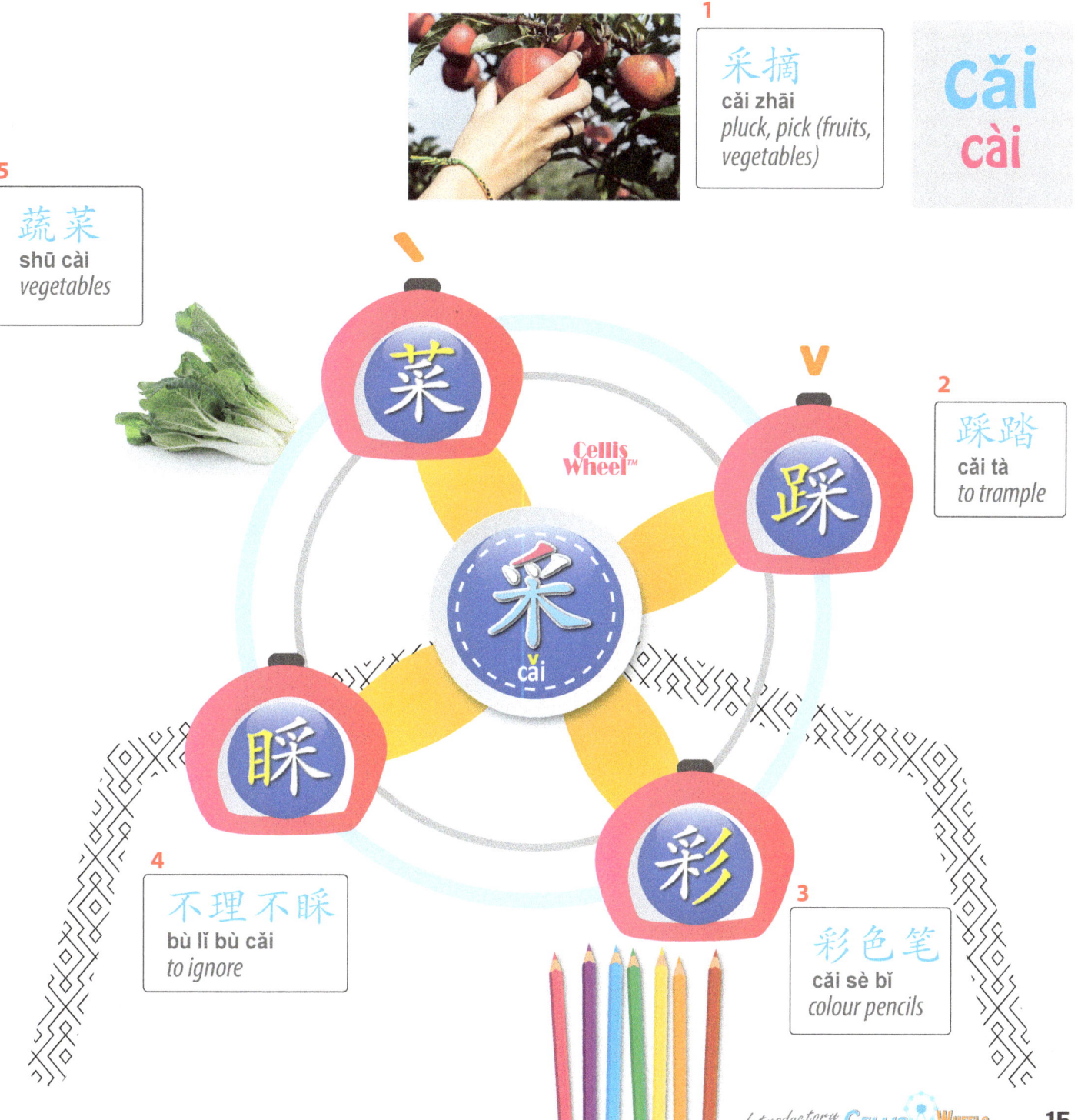

1

采摘
cǎi zhāi
pluck, pick (fruits, vegetables)

cǎi
cài

5

蔬菜
shū cài
vegetables

菜

踩

睬

彩

采
cǎi

Cellis
Wheel™

2

踩踏
cǎi tà
to trample

4

不理不睬
bù lǐ bù cǎi
to ignore

3

彩色笔
cǎi sè bǐ
colour pencils

luó
luō

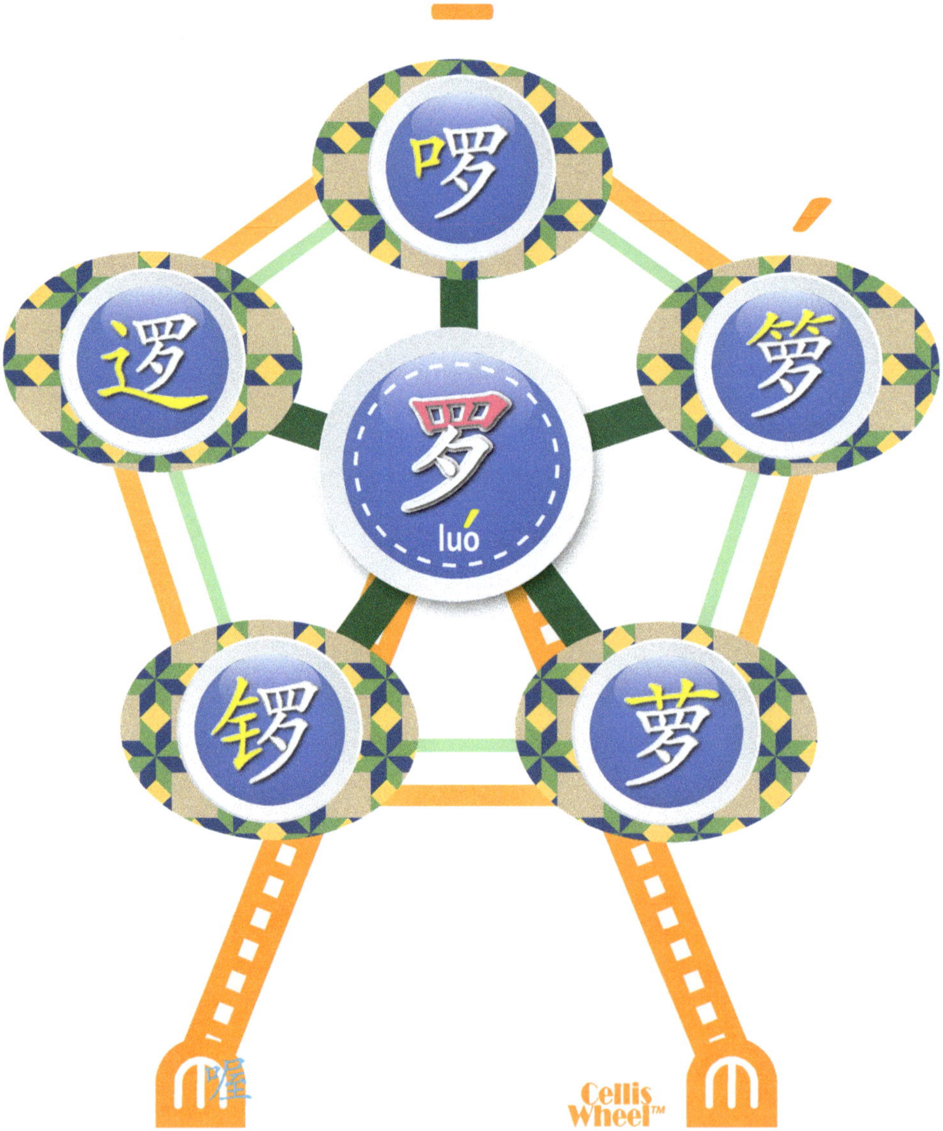

1

罗盘
luó pán
Chinese magnetic compass

2

啰嗦
luō suo
long-winded

3

箩筐
luó kuāng
large woven basket

4

萝卜
luó bo
carrot

5

铜锣
tóng luó
gong

6

逻辑
luó ji
logic

啰

逻

罗
luó

箩

锣

萝

Cellis
Wheel™

16   OSDT

Trick 3   ## OSOT Online Activities

http://bit.ly/2ENXGpZ

LEARN

1. **Listen** to the Chinese pronunciation
2. **Repeat** what you hear
3. **Understand and remember** the meaning of vocabularies through the English translation and picture (if applicable)

FLASHCARDS

1. **Listen** to English translation and **look at** the picture
2. **Recall** the Chinese pronunciation
3. Tap to flip the Flashcard
4. **Listen** to Chinese pronunciation and correct your own pronunciation

MATCH

1. **Revise** all the vocabularies by playing the **Matching Game** in the shortest possible time

Trick 3   **OSDT Online Activities**

http://bit.ly/2EsQSQG

LEARN

1. **Listen** to the Chinese pronunciation
2. **Repeat** what you hear
3. **Understand and remember** the meaning of vocabularies through the English translation and picture (if applicable)

FLASHCARDS

1. **Listen** to English translation and **look at** the picture
2. **Recall** the Chinese pronunciation
3. Tap to flip the Flashcard
4. **Listen** to Chinese pronunciation and correct your own pronunciation

MATCH

1. **Revise** all the vocabularies by playing the **Matching Game** in the shortest possible time

RS
Rhyming Sounds

One or more characters in the wheel has a slight change in sound at the beginning but end the same way. They appear in balls with lighter shade(s) of blue.

Trick 2

1. Learn the **sound of CELL**
2. **Vary the sound** of a multiple when you come across a ball in a **lighter shade of blue.** Note the similarities and differences in the Hanyin pinyin (*e.g. zhong, chong, cong*).

huī
kuī

1
灰色
huī sè
grey

2
诙谐
huī xié
*humorous;
humour*

3
恢复
huī fù
*to recover; restore;
recovery*

kuī

4
头盔
tóu kuī
helmet

恢

诙   灰
     huī

盔

Cells
Wheel™

Cells
Wheel™

lián

jiǎn

lián

练

1

练习
liàn xí
to practise

炼

2

炼钢
liàn gāng
steel-making

jiǎn

拣

东

3

拣选
jiǎn xuǎn
to select

Cellis
Wheel™

Introductory CELLIS WHEELS **21**

zèng
céng
cèng
sēng

曾经
céng jīng
*at one time;
once*

曾
zēng
surname

增加
zēng jiā
increase

憎恨
zēng hèn
detest

赠送
zèng sòng
give for free

蹭车
cèng chē
*ride (on a
bus) without
paying*

僧人
sēng rén
*Buddhist
monk*

Cellis
Wheel™

22   **RS**

1
从前
cóng qián
*in the past;
formerly*

cóng
sǒng
zòng
zhòng

丛
纵 zòng

丛
cóng

牮

怂

众 zhòng

2
丛林
cóng lín
jungle

3
放纵
fàng zòng
*indulge; let
someone have
their own way*

4
大众
dà zhòng
*the public;
the masses*

5
怂恿
sǒng yǒng
*instigate;
egg (someone)
on*

ˇ sǒng

6
牮肩
sǒng jiān
*shrug one's
shoulders*

Cellis Wheel™

Introductory **CELLIS WHEELS** **23**

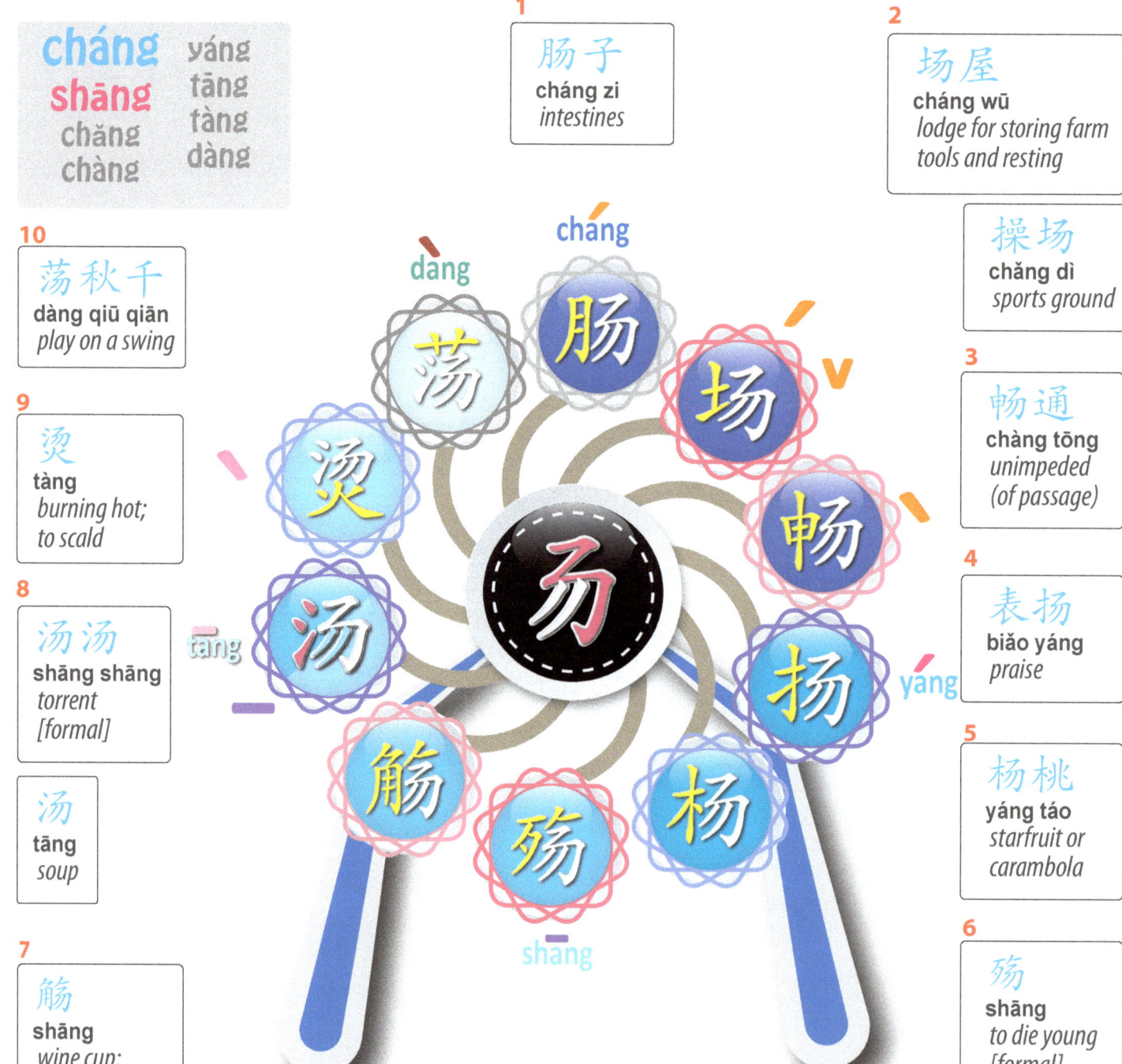

cháng	yáng
shāng	tāng
chǎng	tàng
chàng	dàng

1

肠子
cháng zi
intestines

2

场屋
cháng wū
lodge for storing farm tools and resting

操场
chǎng dì
sports ground

3

畅通
chàng tōng
unimpeded (of passage)

4

表扬
biǎo yáng
praise

5

杨桃
yáng táo
starfruit or carambola

6

殇
shāng
to die young [formal]

7

觞
shāng
wine cup; drinking vessel

8

汤汤
shāng shāng
torrent [formal]

汤
tāng
soup

9

烫
tàng
burning hot; to scald

10

荡秋千
dàng qiū qiān
play on a swing

cháng
dàng
yáng
shāng
tāng

肠 场 畅 扬 杨 殇 汤 烫 荡

 **Trick 3**　　**RS** Online Activities

http://bit.ly/2nRnmK2

LEARN

1. **Listen** to the Chinese pronunciation
2. **Repeat** what you hear
3. **Understand and remember** the meaning of vocabularies through the English translation and picture (if applicable)

FLASHCARDS

1. **Listen** to English translation and **look at** the picture
2. **Recall** the Chinese pronunciation
3. Tap to flip the Flashcard
4. **Listen** to Chinese pronunciation and correct your own pronunciation

MATCH

1. **Revise** all the vocabularies by playing the **Matching Game** in the shortest possible time

OOO
Odd One Out

If there is only one 'Odd One Out (OOO)' that is pronounced differently, it is encased in a grey ball.

 **Trick 2**

1. Learn the **sound of CELL**
2. Take note of the **unique sound(s)** of characters in **grey ball(s)** and compare with the sound of the cell

huí
huái

huái

佪

洄

回
huí

茴

蛔

Cells Wheel™

bià n
bà n

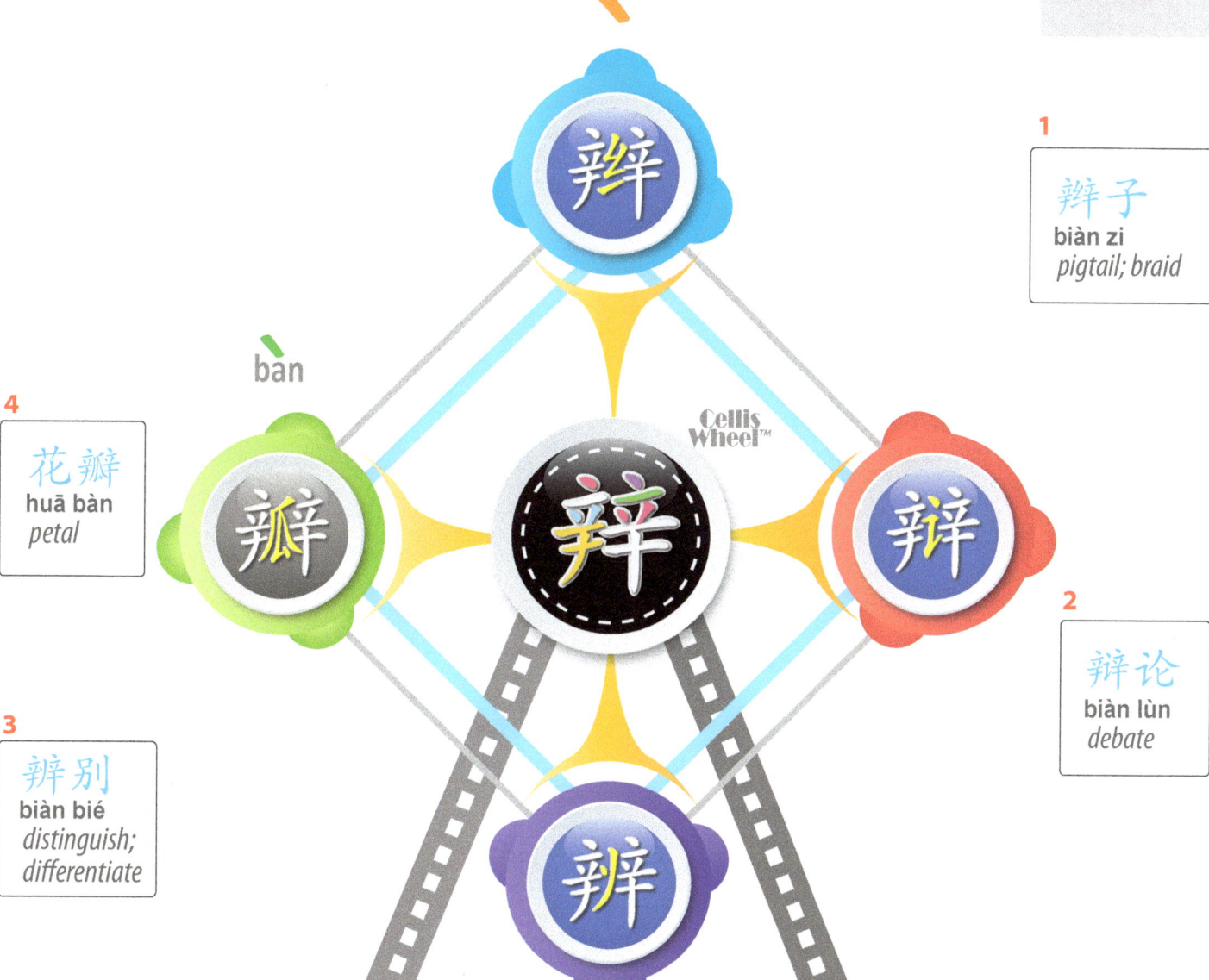

1
辫子
biàn zi
pigtail; braid

2
辩论
biàn lùn
debate

3
辨别
biàn bié
*distinguish;
differentiate*

4
花瓣
huā bàn
petal

bàn

Cellis
Wheel™

000

DS
Different Sounds

If more than one character is pronounced different from those
in blue balls, they reside in orange balls

Trick 2

1. Remember the **sound of CELL**

2DS:

2. Take note of the **second set of sounds** shown
by the **orange balls** and compare with the
sounds of the blue family

3DS:

3. Take note of the **second and third set of
sounds (green balls)** and compare these 3 sets
of sounds

wò
wū
wō

1
屋子
wū zi
house

2
喔
wō
a cock's crow

3
握手
wò shǒu
shake hands

4
龌龊
wò chuò
*filthy;
narrow-minded
[formal]*

6
帷幄
wéi wò
army tent

5
优渥
yōu wò
favourable

wō — 喔
wū — 屋
幄
握
龌
渥

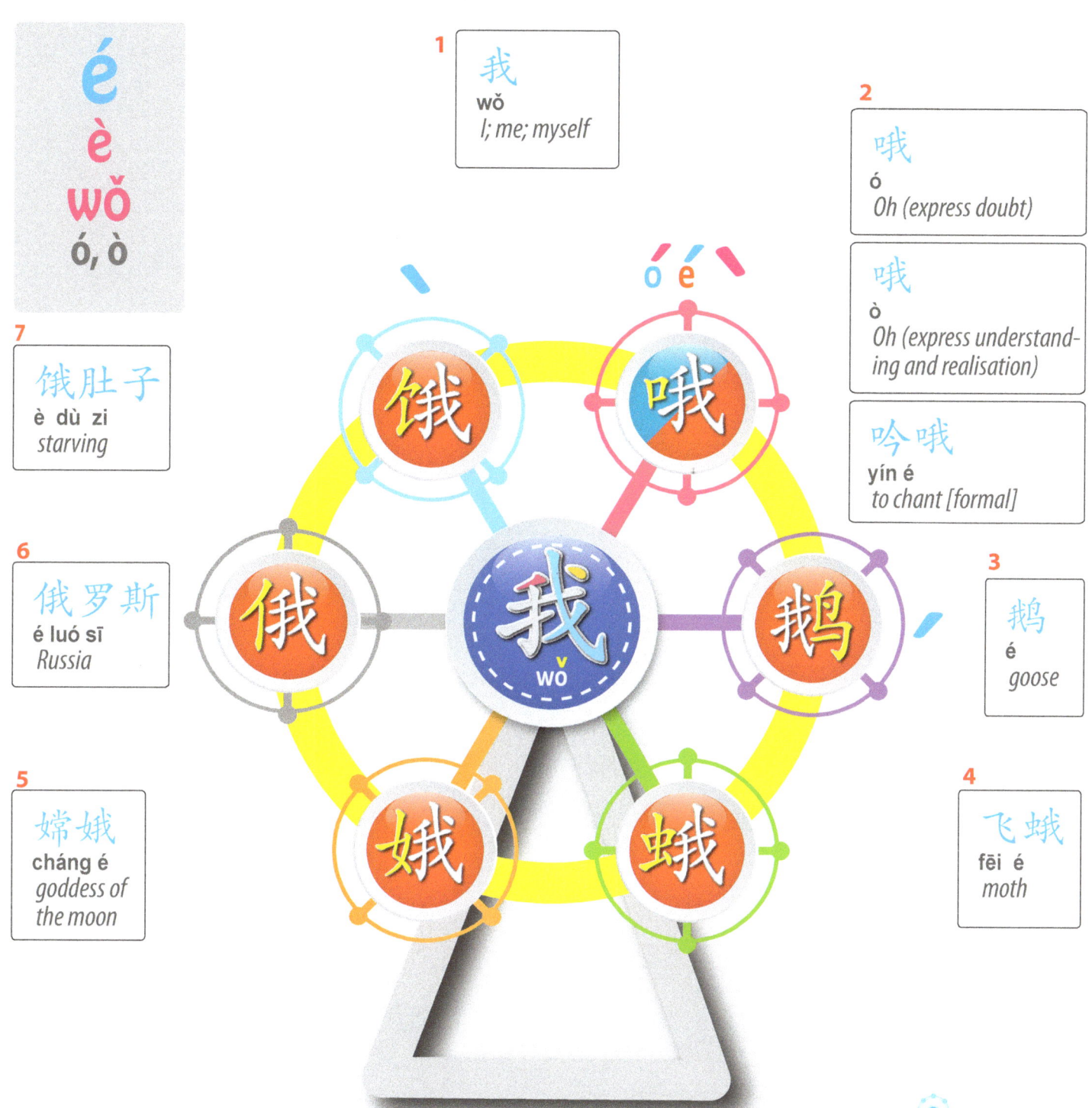

é
è
wǒ
ó, ò

1
我
wǒ
I; me; myself

2
哦
ó
Oh (express doubt)

哦
ò
Oh (express understanding and realisation)

吟哦
yín é
to chant [formal]

3
鹅
é
goose

4
飞蛾
fēi é
moth

5
嫦娥
cháng é
goddess of the moon

6
俄罗斯
é luó sī
Russia

7
饿肚子
è dù zi
starving

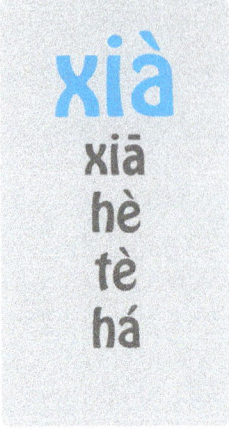

1

下去
xià qù
go down

2

吓人
xià rén
scary

恐吓
kǒng hè
threaten

3

忐忑
tǎn tè
perturbed

4

虾蟆
há ma
toad
(same as
蛤蟆*)*

虾
xiā
prawn

tí
dī
shì
shi, chí

NOTE: Although these pronunciations all end with 'í', they are pronounced differently. Listen to the pronunciation online (see page 38).

1
是 不 是
shì bù shì
*yes or no;
whether or not*

2
汤 匙
tāng chí
soup spoon

钥 匙
yào shi
key

3
主 题
zhǔ tí
*theme;
subject*

5
堤 坝
dī bà
*dykes and
dams*

4
提 防
dī fang
guard against

提 起 来
tí qǐ lái
lift up

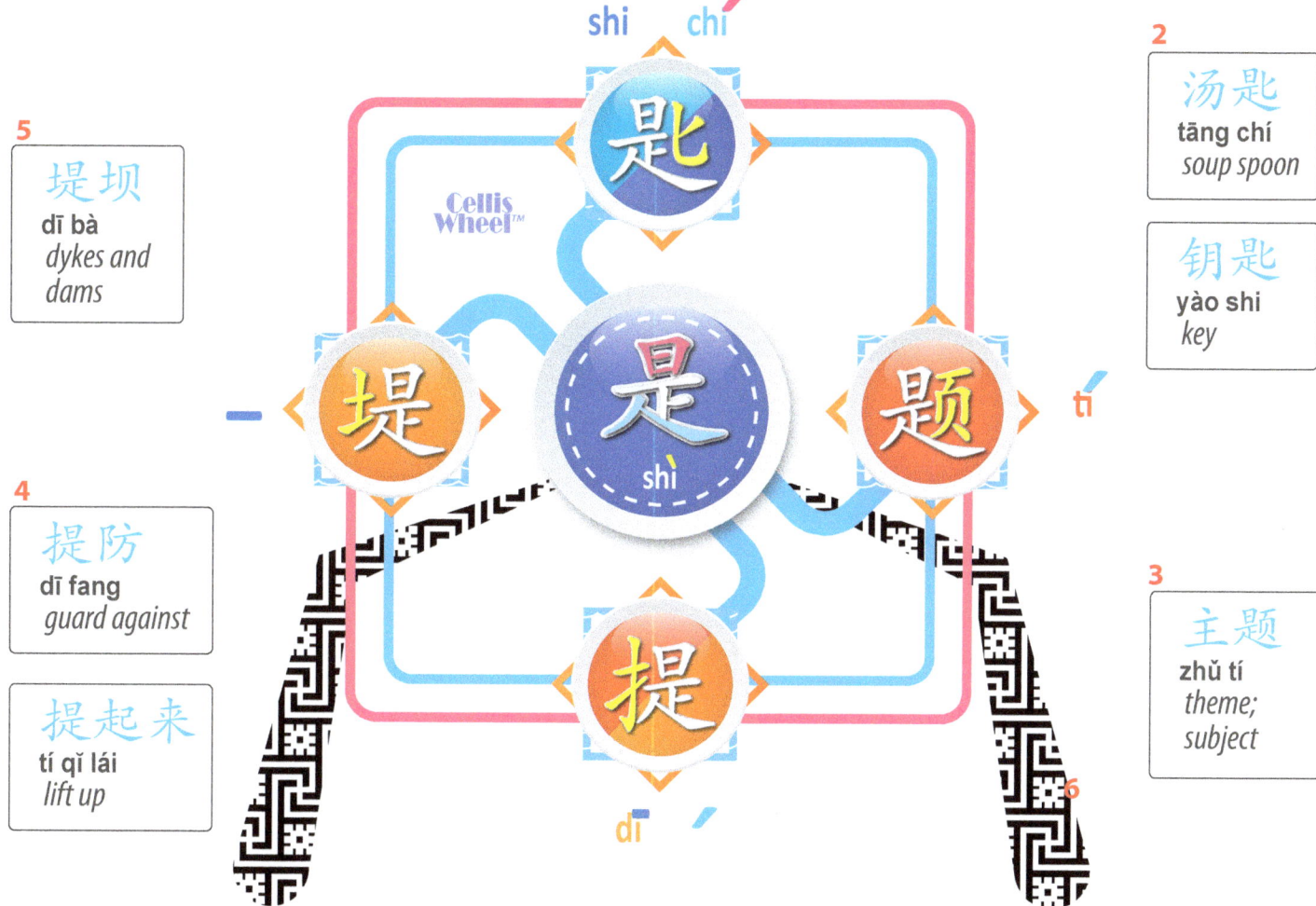

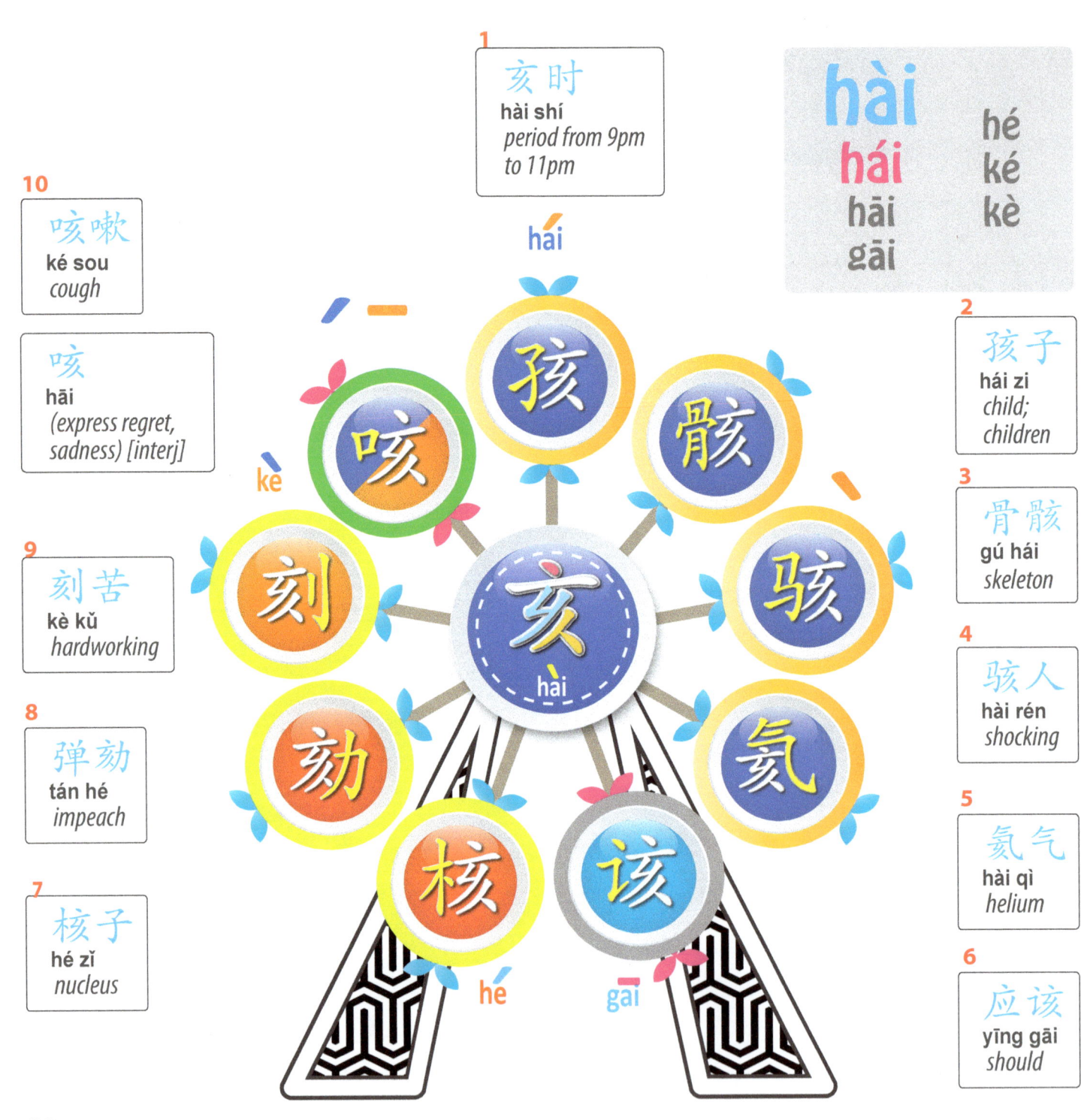

1
亥时
hài shí
period from 9pm to 11pm

hài
hái
hāi
gāi

hé
ké
kè

10
咳嗽
ké sou
cough

咳
hāi
(express regret, sadness) [interj]

9
刻苦
kè kǔ
hardworking

8
弹劾
tán hé
impeach

7
核子
hé zǐ
nucleus

hái

kè

hé

gāi

2
孩子
hái zi
child; children

3
骨骸
gú hái
skeleton

4
骇人
hài rén
shocking

5
氦气
hài qì
helium

6
应该
yīng gāi
should

kāi
xíng
jīng
yán

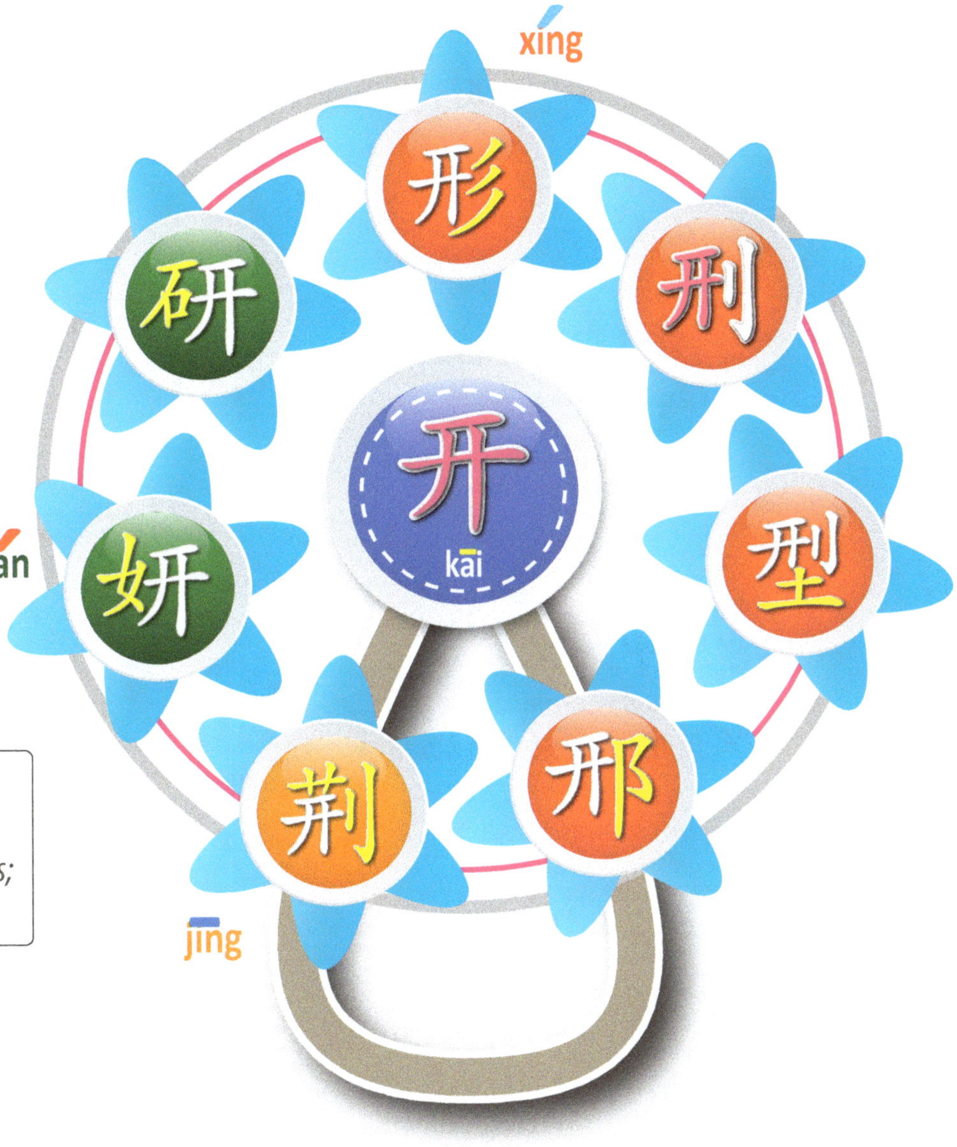

开 kāi

形 xíng

研 yán

妍 yán

刑

型

邢

荆 jīng

1
开始
kāi shǐ
start, begin

2
形状
xíng zhuàng
shape

3
刑罚
xíng fá
punishment

4
型号
xíng hào
model; type

5
邢
xíng
surname

6
荆棘
jīng jí
thistles and thorns; difficulties

7
妍丽
yán lì
beautiful; colourful

8
研究
yán jiū
research

 **Trick 3** **OOO & DS Online Activities**

http://bit.ly/2C4Ya8a

LEARN
1. **Listen** to the Chinese pronunciation
2. **Repeat** what you hear
3. **Understand and remember** the meaning of vocabularies through the English translation and picture (if applicable)

FLASHCARDS
1. **Listen** to English translation and **look at** the picture
2. **Recall** the Chinese pronunciation
3. Tap to flip the Flashcard
4. **Listen** to Chinese pronunciation and correct your own pronunciation

MATCH
1. **Revise** all the vocabularies by playing the **Matching Game** in the shortest possible time

Revision

Recall what you have learnt in the Cellis Wheels.

Consolidate what you have learnt

.

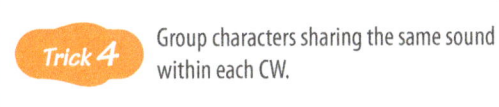

Trick **4** — Group characters sharing the same sound within each CW.

Group character(s) with the same sound

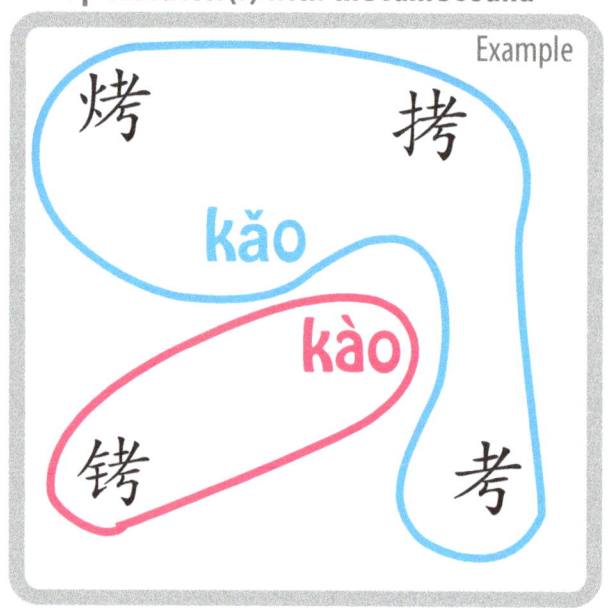

Example

烤　　拷

kǎo

kào

铐　　考

螂　　　　嘟

郎　　láng　　廊

　　　lāng

榔

烂

làn

拦　　兰

　　lán

栏

踩

睬　　　　采

　　cǎi　cài

菜　　　彩

灰　　　　恢
hui　**kui**
诙　　　　盔

练
jiǎn
　　　　炼
liàn
拣

笊　　　啰
luó
罗
luō
锣　　　逻

洄　　　苗
蛔　　**huí**
huái
回　　　伺

辩　　　　辩

biàn

bàn

瓣　　　　辨

握　　　　渥
　　wò
屋　　　　龌
　　wū
　　wǒ
喔　　　　幄

提
tí
题　　　　堤
　　dī
匙　　　　是
　　shì
chí, shi

蛾　　　　鹅
　　é
饿　　　　俄
　　è
我　　　　娥
　　wǒ
哦　　　　
　　ó, ò

赠　　　蹭

zēng
zèng
céng
cèng
sēng

憎　　　增

曾　　　僧

从　　　怂

cóng
zòng
sǒng
zhòng

丛　　　耸

众　　　纵

Answers

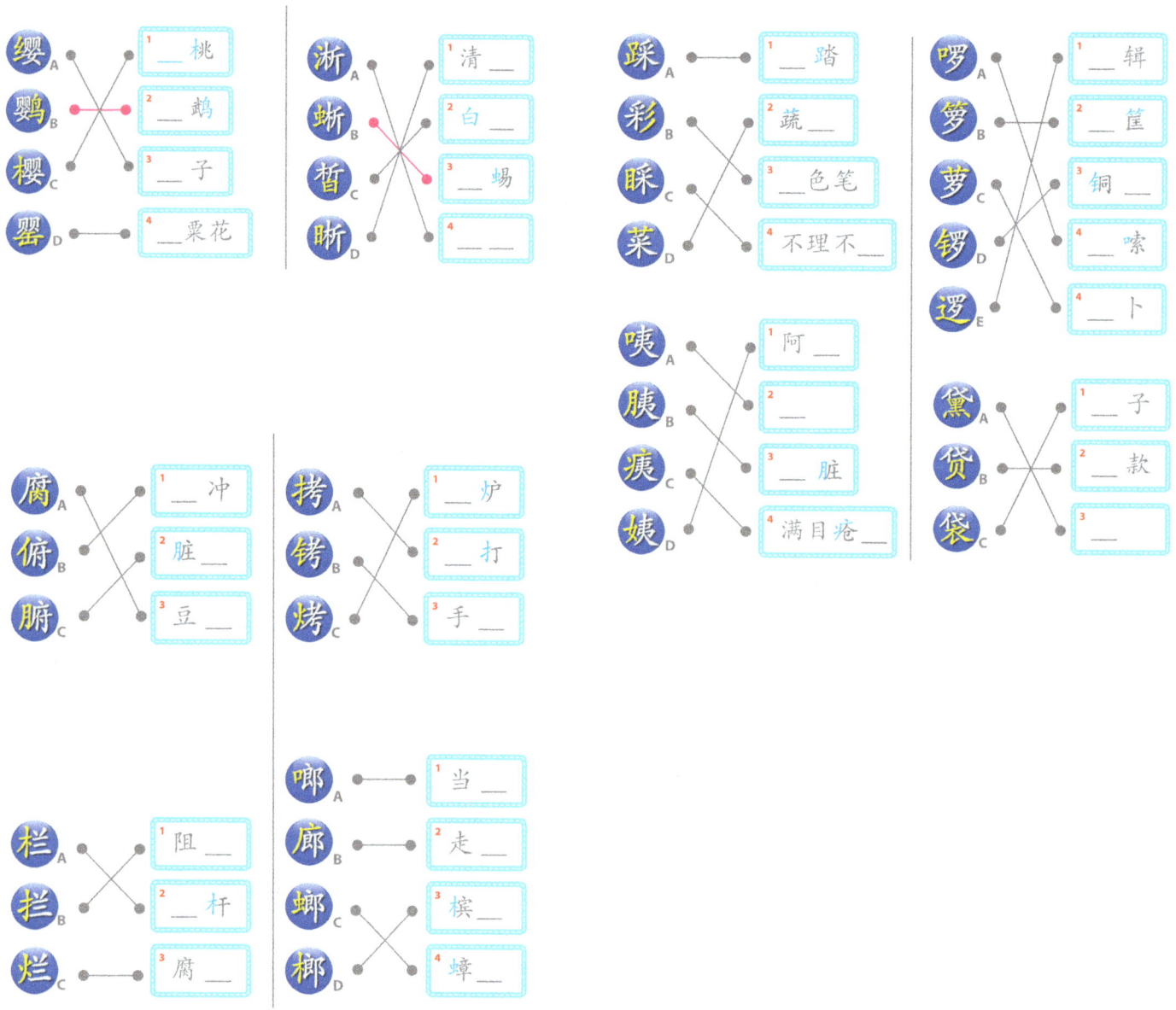

Answers

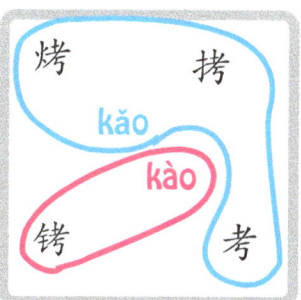

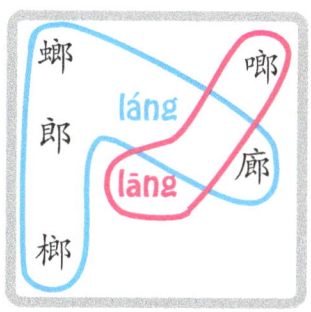

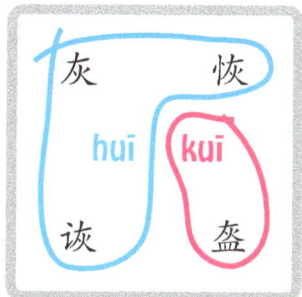

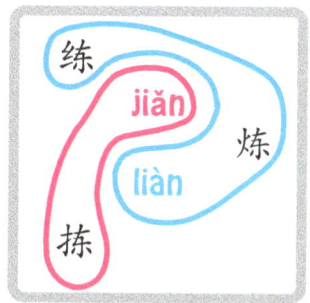

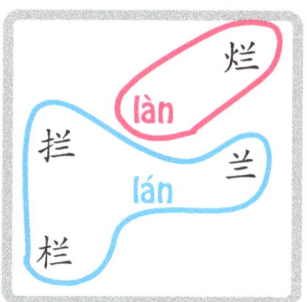

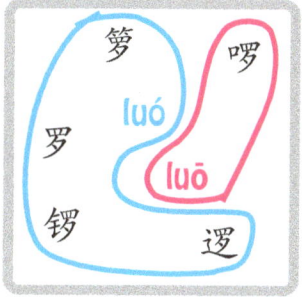

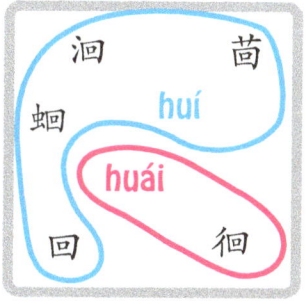

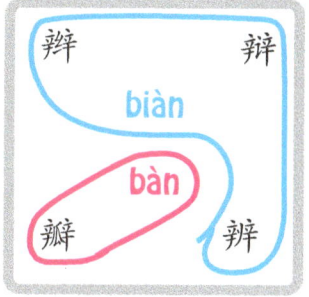

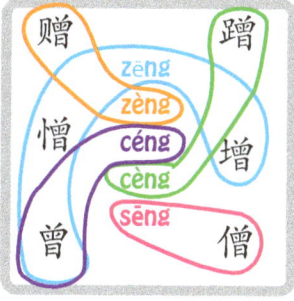

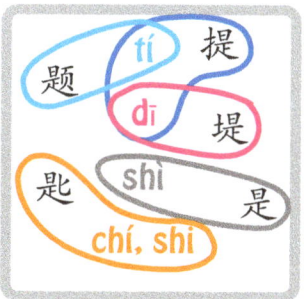

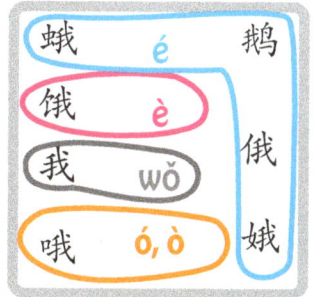